Cape Cod Memories

Karen Choppa

& Mary L. Martin

A CROSSROAD, PROVINCETOWN, CAPE COD, MASS.

DESIGNED BY CHRISTOPHER WREN.

HOLLYHOCK LANE AT PROVINCETOWN ON HISTORIC CAPE COD 27

SEA PINES SCHOOL, EAST BREWSTER, CAPE COD, MASS.

Schiffer Publishing Ltd

4880 Lower Valley Road, Atglen, PA 19310 USA

Published by Schiffer Publishing Ltd.
4880 Lower Valley Road
Atglen, PA 19310
Phone: (610) 593-1777; Fax: (610) 593-2002
E-mail: Info@schifferbooks.com

For the largest selection of fine reference books on this and related subjects, please visit our web site at **www.schifferbooks.com**
We are always looking for people to write books on new and related subjects. If you have an idea for a book please contact us at the above address.

This book may be purchased from the publisher.
Include $3.95 for shipping.
Please try your bookstore first.
You may write for a free catalog.

In Europe, Schiffer books are distributed by
Bushwood Books
6 Marksbury Ave.
Kew Gardens
Surrey TW9 4JF England
Phone: 44 (0) 20 8392-8585; Fax: 44 (0) 20 8392-9876
E-mail: info@bushwoodbooks.co.uk
Website: www.bushwoodbooks.co.uk
Free postage in the U.K., Europe; air mail at cost.

Designed by Mark David Bowyer
Type set in Arrus BT

ISBN: 0-7643-2389-X
Printed in China
1 2 3 4

Contents

1112—Lewis Bay and Englewood Beach, Cape Cod, Mass.

6A-H2739

Introduction

Beware, armchair travelers, for *Cape Cod Memories* may create a constant yearning that only walks along the Cape's streets and coves will satisfy. For those who have already visited the Cape, this book will conjure up recollections of that idyllic vacation. For natives and those fortunate enough to have ever lived there, it will be like reading a letter from home in picture and verse.

Like the images on the wish-you-were-here postcards of vacationers and the day-to-day journal entries of native islanders, *Cape Cod Memories* captures a way of life that is both historic and nostalgic. Over two hundred historic postcards, produced from the early 1900s through the 1950s, paint a picture of a carefree time when life was less hurried and complex, the type of lifestyle that most associate with the Cape.

No one better portrayed that lifestyle than writer and poet Joseph Crosby Lincoln. A native of Cape Cod from a seafaring family, Lincoln developed an intimate understanding of the Cape, its people, and its pull on our imaginations. His words from *Cape Cod Ballads* are interspersed throughout these pages, amid the charming and picturesque images of small towns, quiet beaches, and bustling harbors.

Enjoy!

WYCHMERE HARBOR, HARWICH, CAPE COD, MASS.

42055

"Cape Cod" – the name conjures up myriad sensations like the tangy scent of salt air, the taste of beach plum jelly, the sound of foghorns in the distance, the feel of canvas as sails are hoisted, and the sight of ruby red cranberries floating on a sea of blue. This postcard shows a view of Wychmere Harbor in Harwich, Cape Cod. [Postcard valued at $3-5]

61296

Crosstrees, the Joseph C. Lincoln home at Chatham, overlooks a cove and is accented by the rambling roses so prominent on the Cape. [Postcard valued at $5-7]

From Lincoln's summer residence, views of Cockle Cove and the ocean inspired his poetry and novels. [Postcard valued at $3-5]

128 THE OCEAN FROM JOSEPH C. LINCOLN ESTATE, CHATHAM, CAPE COD, MASS. 111741

Cape Cod

"The dear old Cape! I love it! I love its hills of sand,
The sea-wind singing o'er it, the seaweed on its strand;
The bright blue ocean 'round it, the clear blue sky o'erhead;
The fishing boats, the dripping nets, the white sails filled and spread…."

– From "The Surf Along the Shore"

Long after the wind and waves had carved out the hooked land mass that juts out into the Atlantic Ocean, the Cape got its name. In 1602 an explorer, Bartholomew Gosnold, dropped anchor at the tip, where his ship was soon surrounded by schools of codfish. He named the place Cape Cod for the abundance of codfish he caught that day. Despite later attempts to change it, the name stuck.

In 1620, the legendary *Mayflower* rounded the tip of Cape Cod and anchored in the natural harbor of present-day Provincetown. In the words of one of the Pilgrims, "being thus safely arrived in a good harbor and brought to safe land, they fell upon their knees and blessed the God of Heaven."

At that time, the Cape was a more densely-forested peninsula inhabited by tribes of Wampanoags. They lived in lodges made from saplings and bark tied together with vines and insulated with seaweed. Massasoit, their leader, met with the Pilgrims at Plimoth Plantation in 1621. His welcome opened the door for the many more settlers who followed. Eventually towns would spread from Bourne to Provincetown. One, Mashpee, was the age-old community of the Wampanoags.

In the first part of the twentieth century, Cape Cod became an entity onto itself. Once a peninsula of Massachusetts, it evolved into an island with the completion of the Cape Cod Canal in 1914. Three bridges, two for cars and one for trains, would come to link the two portions up again. As an island, it remains true to itself.

Fishing played a major role in the development of the area as attested to by the Cape's name and the communities of fishing shacks that sprang up along the coastline. This card, postmarked 1942, features fishing shacks at Chatham. [Postcard valued at $4-6]

Henry David Thoreau likened Cape Cod to the "bare and bended arm of Massachusetts: the shoulder is at Buzzard's Bay; the elbow…at Cape Mallebarre; the wrist at Truro; and the sandy fist at Provincetown." You can see the form in this card postmarked 1950. [Postcard valued at $3-5]

A postcard mailed in 1939 shows "Ye Old Town Crier," of Provincetown, whose costume and function can be traced back to Pilgrim days. [Postcard valued at $3-5]

OLD INDIAN CHURCH. MASHPEE. CAPE COD. MASS.

YE OLD TOWN CRIER. PROVINCETOWN. CAPE COD. MASS.

This card is postmarked 1939 and features the oldest religious building on Cape Cod. It is the old Indian Meeting House at Mashpee belonging to the Wampanoags. Built in 1684 with the aid of missionary Richard Bourne, the simple frame structure is surrounded by an ancient burial ground. Today the building houses colorful quilts, each telling a story about a Wampanoag Indian who has passed away. [Postcard valued at $3-5]

The Aptucxet Trading Post, a Pilgrim Dutch trading post in Bourne, speaks of the ancestry of present-day Cape Codders. The original building was destroyed by a hurricane in 1635. What remains today is the reconstructed east room that stands on the site of the original trading post. [Postcard valued at $4-6]

Aptucxet 1627, Pilgrim Dutch Trading Post, Bourne, Cape Cod, Mass.

Cape Cod Canal

"And my heart leaps gaily upward, like the foam upon the sea,
As I watch the breakers tumbling with a roar,
And the ships that dot the azure seem to wave a hail to me,
And to beckon to a wondrous, far-off shore."

– From "The Meadow Road"

Thoughts of a channel connecting Scusset Creek and Manomet River began with the Pilgrims and continued throughout the colonial period. In 1776, George Washington recommended a survey to test the feasibility of a canal, but it wasn't until the twentieth century that the dream was fulfilled.

It took five years (1909-1914) to complete the canal that separated the onetime peninsula of Cape Cod from the rest of Massachusetts. It began as a private enterprise, financed by capitalist August Belmont. The U.S. government purchased the canal in 1928.

The entrance to the Canal is at Buzzard's Bay with its State Pier. Card is postmarked 1942. [Postcard valued at $3-5]

STATE PIER AND ENTRANCE TO CAPE COD CANAL, BUZZARDS BAY, MASS.

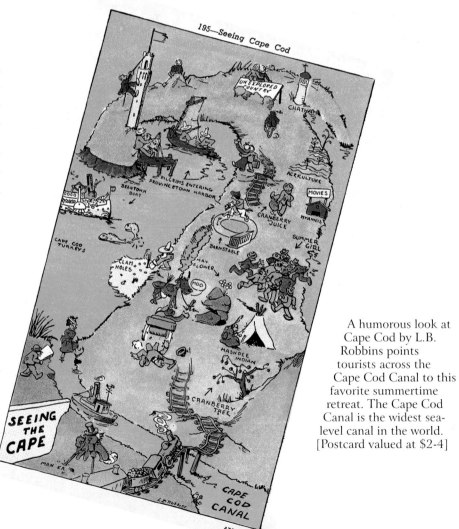

195—Seeing Cape Cod

A humorous look at Cape Cod by L.B. Robbins points tourists across the Cape Cod Canal to this favorite summertime retreat. The Cape Cod Canal is the widest sea-level canal in the world. [Postcard valued at $2-4]

VIEW FROM STATE HIGHWAY, BOATS PASSING THROUGH CAPE COD CANAL.

The Canal shortened the sea trip between Boston and New York by at least sixty miles. Here are two views of ships as they pass through the Canal. One view is taken from the State Highway around 1930, and the other features the steamer from Boston to New York. [Postcards valued at $3-5 each]

153   BOSTON TO NEW YORK STEAMER PASSING THROUGH CAPE COD CANAL, MASS.   108002

It was not unusual for those on the Cape to flock to the Canal's edge at night to watch the Boston-to-New-York steamer pass by. Those on board and those on land would wave to each other while music from the ship's orchestra drifted across the water. [Postcard valued at $4-6]

143   BOSTON TO NEW YORK STEAMER PASSING THROUGH CAPE COD CANAL, MASS.   107997

153   BOSTON TO NEW YORK BOAT BY NIGHT, PASSING THROUGH CAPE COD CANAL, MASS.   5A-H2019

Another nighttime passage of the steamer along the Canal is spotlighted by a full moon. This card is postmarked 1937. [Postcard valued at $4-6]

TORPEDO BOAT DESTROYER PASSING THROUGH CAPE COD CANAL.

Naval vessels also took advantage of the Cape Cod Canal beginning with World War I. Here a torpedo boat destroyer passes through the Canal. [Postcard valued at $7-9]

158 Cape Cod Canal and Bourne Bridge, Cape Cod, Mass.

PHOTO BY HARRISON FISK

8A-H2914

Three bridges were authorized by the government in 1933 and completed in 1935 under the supervision of the Army Corps of Engineers. The total cost was $4,800,000. Here are various views of the Bourne Bridge including a bird's-eye view. A Federal Relief project, the bridge is located at the southern end of the Canal: length 2,684 feet, central span 135 feet above water, width of arch 500 feet, maximum height of steelwork 270 feet above sea-level. [Postcard values: above $4-6; right & below $3-5]

Unusual View of the Bourne Bridge, Cape Cod, Mass.

2

61278

PHOTOGRAPH COPYRIGHTED BY FRED S. HOWARD

157 BIRD'S-EYE VIEW OF THE NEW BOURNE BRIDGE OVER THE CAPE COD CANAL

5A-H731

Railroad and Bourne Bridges Over Cape Cod Canal 122

(Photo by Hicks) 77267

Also at the southern end of the Canal is the railroad bridge. It is one of the largest vertical lift bridges in the world. The cables in the two towers lower the bridge to allow a train to pass over. Afterwards, the span slowly lifts again. This view shows the Bourne Bridge in the background. [Postcard valued at $3-5]

155 View along Cape Cod Canal, Showing Sagamore Bridge

PHOTO BY HARRISON FISK

© E. D. WEST CO.

8A-H2913

The third bridge across the Cape Cod Canal is the Sagamore Bridge that leads travelers onto Route 6, the Cape Cod Highway. A card postmarked 1943 shows the bridge's 1,833-foot span across the Canal. [Postcard valued at $3-5]

THE APPROACH TO THE NEW SAGAMORE BRIDGE, CAPE COD. MASS.

3

The approach to Sagamore Bridge can be quite picturesque on a sunny day especially if there are nearby ships in the Canal. That was the case in 1976 when the Bicentennial Parade of Tall Ships passed through the Canal. The rotary shown in this postcard is soon to be a relic of the past as a new road system is underway. [Postcard valued at $3-5]

SCENIC HIGHWAY LOOKING TOWARD SAGAMORE, CAPE COD. MASS.

42873

Photo by Fred S. Howard

SCENIC HIGHWAY LOOKING TOWARD BOURNE BRIDGE, CAPE COD. MASS.

42872

Photo by Fred S. Howard

Two views from slightly different angles show the scenic highway running along the Canal and the Sagamore and Bourne bridges respectively. [Postcards valued at $3-5 each]

15

Cape Cod Lighthouses

"I've woke ter find the sky a mess of scud and smoky wreath,
A blind wind-devil overhead and hell let loose beneath.
And then ter watch the rollers pound on ledges, bars and rips,
And pray for them that go, O Lord, down ter the sea in ships!
Ter see the lamp, when darkness comes, throw out its shinin' track,
And think of that one gleamin' speck in all the world of black."

– From "The Light-Keeper"

The eight-mile stretch of canal saved ships of all sizes from making the perilous journey around the outer Cape waters where hazardous reefs often took their toll. The need for lighthouses remained, however. They are strung like beads along the neck of land that is Cape Cod and have played many roles, from lifesaver to artist's model.

The darkness of the Cape Cod night is broken by rays of light from these staunch sentinels. The haunting blasts of their foghorns pierce the mists that rise like spirits of the long lost sailors they tried but could not save.

BLUFFS AND BEACH, HIGHLAND LIGHT, CAPE COD, MASS.

The current Highland Light stands sixty-five feet tall atop a cliff 140 feet above sea level. [Postcard valued at $3-5]

The original Highland Light was the first lighthouse on Cape Cod. Its lantern held twenty-four lamps and reflectors fueled by whale oil. Built in 1791 in North Truro, the original wooden structure was torn down sixty years later. A brick lighthouse was erected in 1831. [Postcard valued at $8-10]

HIGHLAND LIGHT, NORTH TRURO.

Highland Light, Cape Cod, Mass.   15

The rays from Highland Light can be seen forty miles at sea. For many years, the first view European immigrants had of America was the beacon from the lighthouse shining a welcome to their new homeland. [Postcard valued at $8-10]

163 *U.S. Wireless Station and Highland Light, North Truro, Cape Cod, Mass.*

5A-H2018

This card of the Highland Light, post-marked 1940, shows the U.S. wireless station erected at the site. Highland Lighthouse's name was officially changed to Cape Cod Light in 1976, but for New Englanders it will always be the Highland Light. [Postcard valued at $5-7]

Nobska Lighthouse is at Woods Hole. The first light was built in 1828. In 1876 it was rebuilt as a brick-lined, cast-iron tower standing forty feet tall. Its light does not revolve, unlike most beacons. Card is post-marked 1929. [Postcard valued at $7-9]

NOBSKA LIGHT, WOODS HOLE.

NOBSKA LIGHT AND BEACH, WOODS HOLE, CAPE COD, MASS.

45840

This postcard shows the beach approach to Nobska Lighthouse with its perch atop a rocky bluff. The light overlooks some of the busiest sea traffic along the Cape. [Postcard valued at $5-7]

Twin lighthouses once warned seaman away from Chatham's treacherous shoals. In 1923 one was moved up the coast to replace the Nauset Lighthouse. In this early 1900s view, the twin lights still stand together. They are flanked by the Mack Monument erected in memory of Captain William Mack, four of his barge's crew members, and seven lifesavers who attempted to rescue them on March 17, 1902. Card is postmarked 1929. [Postcard valued at $8-10]

MACK MONUMENT AND TWIN LIGHTS, CHATHAM.

RACE POINT LIGHT,

A view of Race Point Light from a postcard book mailed in 1929 has the feel of an Edward Hopper
painting, one of the many prominent artists who has had a studio on Cape Cod. [Postcard valued at $6-8]

© EOWEST.
STATE HIGHWAY TO COAST GUARD STATION, PROVINCETOWN, MASS. CAPE COD.

107985

In between the lighthouses, U.S. Lifesaving Service Stations once dotted the forty-mile coastline along the Atlantic beach side of Cape Cod. Lifesavers would patrol the beaches both day and night in search of ships in trouble. Today's U.S. Coast Guard continues the work of those brave men. The state highway into Provincetown appears to lead directly to the Coast Guard station there. [Postcard valued at $3-5]

189—Long Point Light at Tip End of Cape Cod, Provincetown, Mass.

7B-H1368

The current Long Point Light was built in 1875. It stands on the extreme end of Cape Cod at the entrance of Provincetown Harbor. The fog signal building and keeper's house seen here have since been destroyed. Today the Light boasts solar panels installed in the 1980s. Card is postmarked 1953. [Postcard valued at $4-6]

Of the Sea

"The dripping deck beneath him reels,
The flooded scuppers spout the brine;
He heeds them not, he only feels
The tugging of a tightened line."

– From "The Cod Fisher"

With over 500 miles of shoreline, water has played a significant role in the life of Cape Codders from day one. Whether they are a part of the fishing industry or the tourist trade, their life's blood is salty brine.

Seafaring vessels plow watery fields to harvest fish, oysters, lobsters, and clams. Others ferry visitors to and from the Cape or transport goods in the wake of their schooner ancestors. The whalers, the clipper ships filled with silk and porcelain from the Orient, and the abolitionist seamen who smuggled slaves to freedom in Canada may be gone, but their legacy lives on in the literature, lore, and artwork of Cape Cod.

An image from a postcard circa 1935-1940 evokes the poetry of Joseph Lincoln: *"The tired breezes are tucked to rest, In the cloud-beds far away; The waves are pressed to the placid breast, Of the dreaming, gleaming bay; The shoreline swims in a hazy heat, Asleep in the sea and sky, And the muffled beat where the breakers meet, Is a soft, sweet lullaby."* From "At Eventide." [Postcard valued at $2-4]

116

CAPE COD CALLS

"We face four seas," our slogan runs,
Four seas of azure blue,
And o'er them forth to foreign climes
Have sailed good men and true.

Our marshes lie in velvet browns,
Soft shades of russet tan,
And o'er them wheel the white winged gulls
A lone crow in the van.

Our beaches white with high piled dunes,
Where the Dusty Miller clings,
Are foils for the gay clad bather folk
Each recurrent season brings.

We're just a summer playground now,
Our Glories in the past
"Cape Cod Calls" in joyous tones
Long may her prestige last.

—Mabel E. Phinney

175—All Sails Set, Cape Cod, Mass.

PHOTO BY ROGER A. WINTERS

The *Confidence* was captained by H.N. West. The vessel was a bark, a sailing ship of three or more masts, with its aftmost mast fore-and-aft rigged and the others square-rigged. She sailed from Provincetown to many foreign ports of call. [Postcard valued at $5-7]

The Provincetown harbor as seen from Town Hill is where ships like the "Confidence' once called home. [Postcard valued at $4-6]

18 The Harbor from Town Hill, Provincetown, Cape Cod, Mass.

95257

Town Pier, Provincetown, Cape Cod, Mass.

Busy harbor scenes abound on Cape Cod. Here fishing boats dock
at the Town Pier in Provincetown. [Postcard valued at $5-7]

BUSY HARBOR SCENE. WOODS HOLE. CAPE COD. MASS.

Working boats populate the harbor at Woods Hole.
[Postcard valued at $5-7]

119

Greetings from **CAPE COD, MASS.**

8B-H1135

The quintessential Cape Cod fishermen in their oilskins and jumpers even decorate souvenir postcards. [Postcard values: above $4-6; right $3-5; next page $3-5 each]

Fisherman, Cape Cod

11

WHY WORRY? I AM AN OLD MAN, AND HAVE HAD MANY TROUBLES, BUT MOST OF 'EM NEVER HAPPENED

26

"OLD SALT"; CAPE COD, MASS.

WHY WORRY?
191. I am an old man, and have had many troubles,
but most of 'em never happened.

44293

"WHY WORRY?" SAYS UNCLE BILLY,
"KEEP COOL, GO SLOW AND DON'T GET SILLY!"

COPYRIGHT BY H. S. WYER   CAPE COD, MASS.

Fishing Boat, Cape Cod, Mass.   110

(Photo by Hicks)   76258

A fishing boat awaits its crew in a sun-dappled harbor.
[Postcard valued at $4-6]

Mackerel Fishing Fleet making ready for the season, Provincetown, Cape Cod, Mass.

Cod and mackerel were important food fish, and Cape Cod fishing fleets harvested the Atlantic for both.
Here the fishing fleet is making ready for the season at Provincetown. [Postcard valued at $4-6]

170—Fishing Shacks, Cape Cod, Mass.

4B-H946

Fishing Shanty, Cape Cod, Mass.   119

(Photo by Hickl)   76287

Fishing Shacks at Chatham, Cape Cod, Mass.

During high tide, fishing shacks and shanties "wade" in the water on their wooden "legs."
[Postcards valued at $4-6 each]

9B-H1386

A fisherman's gear includes his lines, roping and anchors. [Postcard valued at $4-6]

DRYING FISHING NETS ALONG THE SHORE OF PROVINCETOWN. CAPE COD, MASS.

Common sights along Cape Cod's shores have been fish and fishing nets drying in the sun. Here they are seen in Provincetown Harbor. [Postcard valued at $4-6]

A STURDY CRAFT

10

"When I mend my nets by the foamin' sea, / Them little bare feet trot there with me, / And a shrill little voice I love 'll say: / 'Dran'pa, spin me a yarn ter-day.'" From "Little Bare Feet." [Postcard valued at $3-5]

Greetings from Cape Cod, Mass.

HELPING GRANDPA

What lessons from the sea
there come,
From its immensity;
Its mystery, horizons far,
Breathe forth eternity.

Along the highways of the
deep,
On wide expanse of sea;
I watch the ships go sailing by
And think of Galilee.
—*Rev. H. F. Huse*

116—Digging Little Neck Clams, Cape Cod, Mass.

8B-H1133

Tides reveal another bounty from the Cape's shores: clams dug up from the wet sand. Card is postmarked 1950. [Postcard valued at $2-4]

"Happy as a Klam on Kape Kod," proclaims a humorous card post-marked 1944. The greeting on the back suggests the sender had gone to the Cape for health reasons. Hopefully the card's sentiment on front meant he was enjoying a full recovery there. [Postcard valued at $2-4]

It's not always sunshine and ocean breezes. Sitting in front of their shanties, clam diggers face the tedious task of shucking. [Postcard valued at $9-11]

CLAM DIGGERS AND SHANTIES 1469

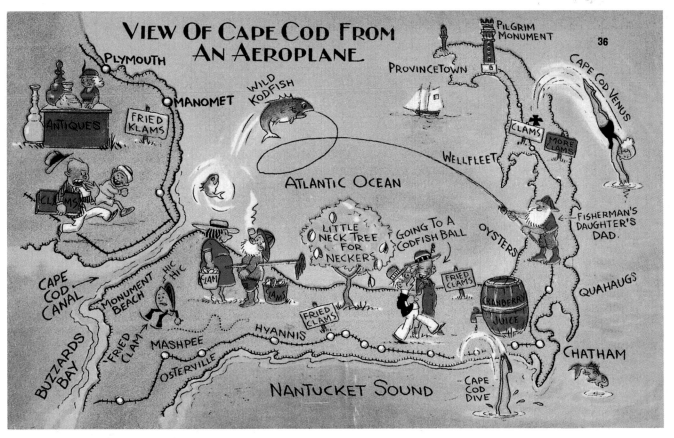

Yet another humorous postcard indicates how synonymous clams were to Cape Cod. Note the "Little Neck Tree for Neckers" in the lower center of the card and numerous mentions of fried clams including one little character (lower left) of a drunken clam, a different type of "fried." [Postcard valued at $2-4]

63:—LOBSTER FISHERMEN, CAPE COD, MASS.

47827

Lobster was once so plentiful and commonplace on the Cape that it was used to fertilize fields and bait hooks. Lobstermen adorn the piers along Cape Cod with their colorful buoys, characteristic lobster traps, and miles of line. [Postcard valued at $4-6]

46

Oyster Houses and Fishing Shacks on Cape Cod, Mass.

70 770

Oyster houses share the Cape Cod shoreline with fishing shacks. [Postcard valued at $4-6]

A gullible outsider might believe oystering is as easy as picking them off an oyster tree (lower left) as this satirical postcard implies. The card is postmarked 1949. [Postcard valued at $2-4]

This black-and-white postcard shows just how important the sea has been to the Cape Cod way of life where the natives may as well have webbed feet and you can fish from your window, reeling the cod right into the frying pan. [Postcard valued at $5-7]

Of the Land

"Now the crowd of cranb'r'y pickers, every mornin' as they pass,
Makes a feller think of turkey, with the usual kind of sass,
Till a roguish face a-smilin' 'neath a bunnit or a hat,
Makes him stop and think of somethin' that's a good deal sweeter'n that;
And the lightsome girlish figger trippin', skippin' down the lane,
Fills his mem'ry full of sunshine, but it's sunshine mixed with rain,
For, yer see, it sets him dreamin' of Septembers that he knew
When he went a cranb'r'y pickin' and a girl went with him, too."

– From "September Mornin's"

A large supply of this country's cranberries comes from the bogs of southeastern Massachusetts. It wasn't until sugar became plentiful to temper the cranberry's puckering taste that the fruit began to be widely harvested on Cape Cod. Before machinery, cranberries were picked with long-toothed scoops. These crimson jewels are processed into a variety of delightful products.

Farmland is also found throughout the Cape. Much of the harvest once was taken to gristmills to be ground into flour or meal. These mills sprang up along the streams; the first waterwheel on Cape Cod began turning in 1654.

Where there were no streams, windmills took their place in providing power. They stood like cloud-capped giants across the landscape, waving their whirling arms. Besides grinding grain, the windmills along the marshes were used to draw up seawater into vats for drying. By the 1830s the salt works were a major industry in all the towns along the Cape. After its heyday, the wood from the dismantled salt vats took new shapes, such as windmills and barns.

Other colonial industries came and went as well, from candle-dipping to cloth weaving. There were vast strawberry beds, shoe factories, and glass works. Oil, meat, blubber, and bone were rendered from the whales dragged onto the beaches. Cape Codders had a penchant for seeing a need and filling it. Taking a cue from the Wampanoags, they even tried producing house insulation from seaweed, which was a short-lived venture.

139 HARVESTING CAPE COD CRANBERRIES, CAPE COD, MASS.   123575

In the 1800s, harvesting cranberries was a big social event that brought everyone to the bogs. In winter they would gather again to skate on the bogs that had been flooded to protect the tender vines. [Postcard valued at $5-7]

Many an unknowing outsider has thought cranberries grow on trees like cherries. L.B. Robbins imagined a "Wonderful Cranberry Tree" (upper left) obviously grafted so that it bears not only cranberries but cranberry sauce and juice, too! This humorous card is postmarked 1952. [Postcard valued at $2-4]

1A38

Over the years, water wheels at Mill Pond in West Brewster have powered everything from shoe to furniture factories. The old gristmill there was built in 1873 using boards from a dismantled saltworks. [Postcard valued at $3-5]

107 OLD EASTHAM MILL, CAPE COD, MASS.

4A-H2042

Originally erected in Plymouth in 1688, this mill was later dismantled and shipped across the bay where it was finally erected again in Eastham in 1793. Much like a ship's sails, the arms of the Old Eastham Mill caught the wind to "fill the hopper and give the lift-wheel a spin." The card is postmarked 1935. [Postcard valued at $3-5]

While a few mills have been restored and today operate primarily for the tourist trade, most have deteriorated or melted back into their surroundings. [Postcard valued at $3-5]

THE OLDEST WINDMILL ON CAPE COD.

166—Making Hay on Cape Cod

PHOTO BY CAPE COD PORTFOLIO   1B-H1831

The grains grown inland on the Cape were milled or used as fodder. Joseph Lincoln reminisced: *"Summer nights at Grandpa's – ain't they soft and still! Just the curtains rustlin' on the window-sill; And the wind a-blowin', warm and wet and sweet – Smellin' like the meadows or the fields of wheat…."* From "Summer Nights at Grandpa's." [Postcard valued at $2-4]

106—Picturesque Scene on Cape Cod, Mass.

1C-H1330

With the decline of the windmills, the millwright became a profession of the past. No more were his handmade peg wheels, giant wooden gears, and massive spindles needed. The millwright went the way of the saltworkers, shuckers, coopers, and weavers. [Postcard valued at $3-5]

And Still They Come

"But when my memory wanders down to the dear old home
I hear, amid my dreaming, the seething of the foam,
The wet wind through the pine trees, the sobbing crash and roar,
The mighty surge and thunder of the surf along the shore."
                                    – From "The Surf Along the Shore"

For hundreds of years travelers from all over have escaped to Cape Cod for its rustic lifestyle and natural beauty. Even in the days of the Wampanoags, the Indians would leave their homes in the interior to enjoy summer in makeshift camps along the shore.

Cape Cod offers visitors a variety of activities from sailing and water sports to sight-seeing and the arts. The shore routes on Cape Cod are lined with quaint houses, village greens, antique shops, and galleries. A practical people, Cape Codders have "gone with the flow," developing a tourist economy.

BATHING BEACH, ONSET BAY, MASS.

171. SURF BATHING, CAPE COD, MASS.

Bathing Beach and Shore Line to Nobska Light, Woods Hole, Cape Cod, Mass.

In wonderful old cards, bathers cavort in the waves on Cape Cod. "Bathing" not swimming was about all one could do in the waterlogged woolen bathing suits of the day. Cards are postmarked 1929 and 1926 respectively. [Postcard values: top $6-8; bottom $5-7]

Many sandy stretches of beach are tucked into the little nooks and crannies that make up the Cape Cod shoreline. This card postmarked 1947 shows the bathing beach and shoreline approach to Nobska Light. [Postcard valued at $4-6]

Bathers at Craigville Beach, Cape Cod, Mass.   H6

As a youth, John F. Kennedy considered Craigville Beach near Hyannis his favorite. This card of Craigville Beach is post-marked 1943. [Postcard valued at $4-6]

Craigville Beach is a family beach, where folks gather by day to swim and by night to fish. Card is postmarked 1953. [Postcard valued at $3-5]

1110—Craigville Beach, Cape Cod, Mass.

7B-H1296

Bath Houses and Beach at Craigville Beach, Cape Cod, Mass.   H7

66011

Cars park along both sides of the access road to Craigville Beach. Those shown here are parked next to the bathhouses. Card is postmarked 1949. [Postcard valued at $4-6]

NEW STATE ROAD ALONG THE BEACH, PROVINCETOWN, CAPE COD, MASS.

42101

A view from along the beach road at Provincetown calls to mind these words by Lincoln: "*I see upon the sand-dunes the beach grass sway and swing; / I see the whirling sea-birds sweep by on graceful wing; / I see the silver breakers leap high on shoal and bar ,/ And hear the bell-buoy tolling his lonely note afar.*" From "The Surf Along the Shore." [Postcard valued at $3-5]

6B-H1377

Accommodations with a water view and beach area are always the most popular. This card of Swifts Beach is postmarked 1956. [Postcard valued at $4-6]

On the Beach at Falmouth Heights, Cape Cod, Mass.

(C) HOWARD

One of the first planned resort areas was in Falmouth Heights in the 1870s that consisted of a cluster of cottages. Today its beaches and piers still welcome summer visitors. [Postcard valued at $3-5]

9-2126

The vastness of glistening beaches, towering dunes, and cloudless skies have a way of putting a visitor's cares into perspective. [Postcard valued at $2-4]

The greeting on this card postmarked 1953 says it all about Cape Cod's beaches: "Finally found the water – Fine place – Weather is on my side also…." Card is postmarked 1953. [Postcard valued at $3-5]

165—One of the Many Bathing Beaches, Cape Cod, Mass.

© CURT TEICH & CO., INC.

7B-H80

Summer Smiles Along a Sunny Cape Cod Shore

Sailing Under Sunny Summer Skies   Cape Cod, Mass,

Summer on Cape Cod does more than smile, as this card implies, it absolutely grins from ear to ear along the curving arc of beaches. Card is postmarked 1942. [Postcard valued at $4-6]

Leaving the shore behind, pleasure boats sail in harbors, coves, bays, and sounds. [Postcard valued at $3-5]

5B-H864

The sails of a windmill in the background mimic the sails of this boat cruising
along the Cape's shoreline. [Postcard valued at $3-5]

304—The Harbor, Falmouth, Cape Cod, Mass.

View of the Harbor, Hyannis on Cape Cod, Mass.

More than sail-powered vessels fill Cape Cod's harbors such as these in Falmouth and the rowboat heading homeward into Hyannis Harbor. [Postcards valued at $4-6 each]

SCARGO LAKE, DENNIS, CAPE COD, MASS.

42060

GLIMPSE OF CRYSTAL LAKE, ALONG CHATHAM ROAD, ORLEANS.

Not all water resort areas are along the outer shorelines of the Cape. Tree-lined Sargo Lake in Dennis and Crystal Lake in Orlean provide additional water attractions. [Postcard values: left $2-4; right $7-9]

Idlewood Lake with its old-time refreshment booth and boat landing was another alternative to saltwater recreation. [Postcard valued at $4-6]

REFRESHMENT BOOTH & BOAT LANDING, IDLEWOOD LAKE, HAMILTON & WENHAM, MASS,

Summer Time on Old Cape Cod

A fuel station for boats anchors the end of this pier. [Postcard valued at $4-6]

185—Wharf Scene, Provincetown, Cape Cod, Mass.

90770-N

With an abundance of natural beauty and rustic charm, it is no wonder that Cape Cod has attracted artists for generations. Still teeming with local color, artists come to transfer these scenes to canvas. This artist is capturing a wharf scene in Provincetown. [Postcard valued at $3-5]

189—*School of Artists on Beach at Provincetown, Cape Cod, Mass.*

In 1901, painter Charles Hawthorne opened the Cape Cod School of Art in Provincetown. American Impressionists were among the first to be inspired by the Cape's landscape. [Postcard valued at $4-6]

Local town streets like those of Onset impart a special look to Cape Cod, and visitors there find an array of shops, restaurants, and sights. Card is postmarked 1939. [Postcard valued at $5-8]

ONSET, CAPE COD, MASS.

photo by Fred S. Howard

214—Town Parking Pier, Onset, Cape Cod, Mass.

6B-H1369

Not a fishing pier but the town's "parking pier" in Onset reveals Onset and Wicket Islands in the background. This card is postmarked 1949. [Postcard valued at $4-6]

183 Main Street, Orleans, Cape Cod, Mass.

5B-H874

A typical Main Street scene in mid-twentieth century Cape Cod with its grocery store and mom-and-pop shops. This scene was shot in Orleans, and the card is postmarked 1952. [Postcard valued at $8-10]

Commercial Street looking West, Provincetown, Cape Cod, Mass.

The "Boat to Boston" sign hints that this is a street scene from Cape Cod, specifically, Provincetown. [Postcard valued at $9-11]

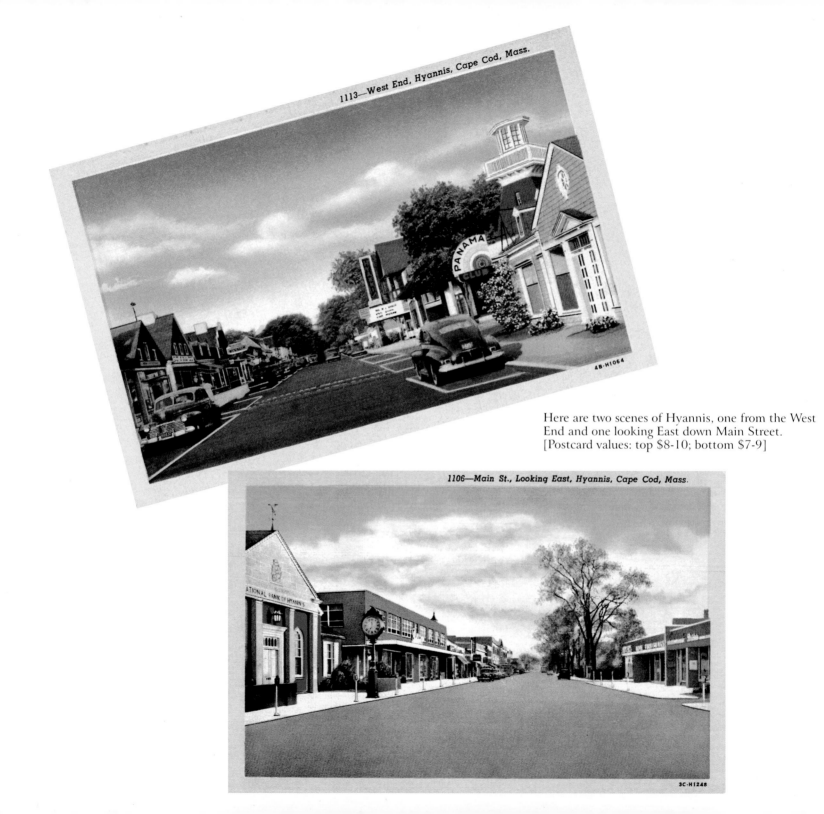

1113—West End, Hyannis, Cape Cod, Mass.

4B-H1064

Here are two scenes of Hyannis, one from the West End and one looking East down Main Street.
[Postcard values: top $8-10; bottom $7-9]

1106—Main St., Looking East, Hyannis, Cape Cod, Mass.

3C-H1248

5

TYPICAL STREET IN A CAPE COD VILLAGE. CAPE COD. MASS.

©HOWARD

Some of the prettiest street scenes are along the Old King's Highway. Originally a Wampanoag trail, the Old King's road stretched from the village of Bourne to Provincetown, but today King's Highway generally refers to Route 6A that stretches along the North shore from Sandwich to Orleans. [Postcard valued at $6-8]

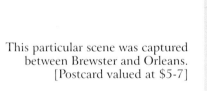

This particular scene was captured between Brewster and Orleans. [Postcard valued at $5-7]

PHOTO BY HARRISON FISK

116   ROSE BLOSSOM TIME ON CAPE COD, MASS.

6A-H1815

55

105—Quaint Homes on the Kings Highway, Cape Cod, Mass.

4A-H1471

The highway is lined with houses dressed in clapboard, shingles, and shutters, strung together with stone and picket fences, and wrapped in climbing roses. [Postcard values: left $5-7; below $4-6]

134   A BEAUTY SPOT, CAPE COD, MASS.

4A-H814

Street Scene, Route 6, Cape Cod, Mass.

102

(Photo by Hicks)

76251

Elms along the King's Highway near Yarmouth were planted in 1840 by Amos Otis, a local historian. They grew to arch gracefully across the road and supply much-welcomed shade in the heat of summer. Card is post-marked 1949. [Postcard valued at $3-5]

PHOTO BY HARRISON FISK

6A-H1816

Traveling the roads of Cape Cod is like peeling back layers of time. Eighteenth-century inns are juxtaposed next to contemporary art galleries, a roadside stand selling beach plum jelly nestles near a nineteenth-century general store, and everywhere is the traditional Cape Cod style house. This scene is from Bass River on Route 28 between Hyannis and Chatham. [Postcard valued at $4-6]

Also along Route 28 that skirts the southern coastline, the Cape Playground near Hyannis attracted visitors with promises of shuffle-board, table tennis, horseshoes, badminton, bocce ball, and refreshments. [Postcard valued at $4-6]

180 THE CAPE PLAYGROUND, ROUTE 28, NEAR HYANNIS, MASS., CAPE COD.   1178

The Oldest House in Provincetown, Cape Cod, Mass. 48

23

Shops abound along Cape Cod routes. This earlier postcard of "The Oldest House in Provincetown" states that the structure is "picturesque, rambling, gracefully weathered by age" and "the oldest building on the tip of the Cape." A few years later, another card postmarked 1932 shows the building converted into a hooked rug shop on one end with a ship model shop on the other. [Postcards valued at $3-5 each]

131   THE OLDEST HOUSE IN PROVINCETOWN, CAPE COD, MASS.

3986-29

Auction on the Cape, Cape Cod, Mass.

What can't be purchased in Cape Cod shops may be had at antique and estate auctions.
[Postcard valued at $6-8]

SAMUEL DE CHAMPLAIN TABLET AT CHATHAM, CAPE COD, MASS.

Variety and history are the key words for sight-seeing on
Cape Cod. A plaque and stone commemorate the visit of
French explorer Samuel de Champlain who mapped
Nauset harbor in 1605. [Postcard valued at $3-5]

111739

186— PILGRIM MEMORIAL MONUMENT, PROVINCETOWN,

CAPE COD, MASS.

The Pilgrim Memorial Monument in Provincetown stands on Town Hill in Provincetown. It was erected to commemorate the landing of the Pilgrims at Cape Cod in 1620; their adoption of the "Compact of the Government," the first charter of a democratic government in the world's history; the birth of Peregrine White, the first white child born in New England; as well as the "entire train of events which preceded the settlement of Plymouth." [Postcard values: left $3-5; right $4-6]

PILGRIM MEMORIAL MONUMENT, AND BAS RELIEF TABLET,

PROVINCETOWN, MASS.

191 Waterfront, Provincetown, Cape Cod, Mass.

5B-H868

The Pilgrim Memorial rises 252 feet above the town as seen from this waterfront view postmarked 1951. [Postcard valued at $3-5]

A bird's-eye view of Provincetown from atop the Pilgrim Memorial. [Postcard valued at $4-6]

15 LOOKING EAST FROM PILGRIM MEMORIAL MONUMENT, PROVINCETOWN, CAPE COD, MASS. 52336

A stone marker in Provincetown notes the first landing place of the Pilgrims. [Postcard valued at $2-4]

106. THE OLDEST WINDMILL ON CAPE COD.

58245

To fuel the tourist trade, all sorts of oddities have been highlighted throughout the Cape, such as the oldest windmill located between Hyannis and Chatham. [Postcard valued at $3-5]

HYANNIS THEATRE.

The old Hyannis Theatre stands out with its distinctly Tudor architectural elements. Card is postmarked 1929. [Postcard valued at $6-8]

112 THE CAPE PLAYHOUSE, DENNIS, CAPE COD, MASS.

6A-H2736

Old Nobscusett Meeting House from Barnstable was moved to Dennis and became the Cape Play House, still complete with old oak pews for seating. Since the very first production , *The Guardsman* starring Basil Rathbone, cast members have entertained islanders and summer visitors alike. Card is postmarked 1937. [Postcard valued at $3-5]

217:-CAPE PLAYHOUSE, DENNIS

CAPE COD, MASS.

50436

Such stars as Robert Montgomery, Henry Fonda, and then-usher Bette Davis got their start at the Cape Play House, giving it the nickname, "Cradle of the Stars." It is reputed to be the oldest professional summer theater. [Postcard valued at $4-6]

Cape Cinema, Dennis, Cape Cod, Mass.

Today the Cape Cinema in Dennis presents documentaries and art films, but the art isn't limited to the big screen. The interior boasts a mural designed by Rockwell Kent. Outside (right), a landscape artist has created a floral masterpiece. [Postcard values: above $4-6; opposite page $3-5]

132 GARDENS AT THE CINEMA, CAPE COD, MASS.

4A-H2040

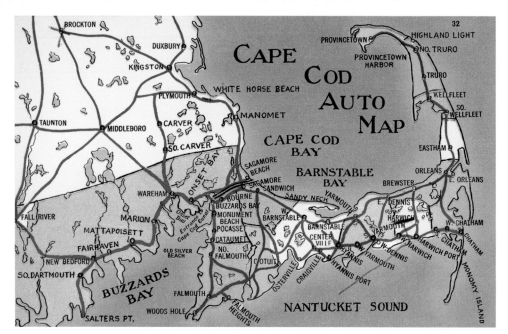

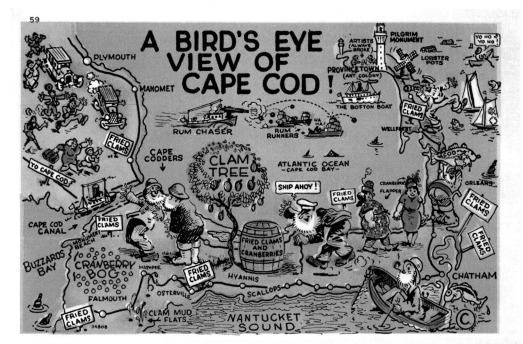

With so much to do and see in Cape Cod, it's no wonder that thousands of postcards are mailed from there each summer. [Postcard values: above left & right $2-4; below left $3-5; opposite page $3-5 each]

301—The Lighthouse Inn, West Dennis, Cape Cod, Mass.

4B-H951

From the most humble of beginnings in 1644, inns have grown and prospered throughout the Cape. Tourist accommodations range from elegant, cliff-top resorts to beachside cottages to B&B's in the heart of villages. At the Lighthouse Inn in West Dennis, a stiff breeze off Nantucket Sound unfurls a beachfront flag. The Inn has been in the same family now since 1938. [Postcard valued at $4-6]

The columned portico at the entrance to the Melrose Inn was needed to protect the writer of this postcard from "the cold Northeast wind" that was "not so good for fishing." The greeting was postmarked in 1949. [Postcard valued at $4-6]

182—The Melrose Inn, Harwichport, Cape Cod, Mass.

8A-H2920

190—The Belmont, West Harwich By-The-Sea, Cape Cod, Mass.

5A-H1964

HOTEL BELMONT, WEST HARWICH

Expansive lawns graced the grounds of the Hotel Belmont in West Harwich By-the-Sea. Its wrap-around porch provided respite from the sun. Cards were postmarked 1940 and 1929 respectively. [Postcard values: top $4-6; bottom $7-9]

Two views of the Terrace Gables in Falmouth Heights. The facility promoted itself as having a bracing breeze at all times, sea-bathing averages of over 70° with no undertow, of being outside the "thunderstorm belt," of having no flies or mosquitoes, and offering "unexcelled cuisine," golf, fishing, and sailing. [Postcard values: top $5-7; bottom $4-6]

Terrace Gables, Falmouth Heights, Cape Cod. Mass.

© HOWARD

Terrace Gables Hotel, Falmouth Heights, Mass. Cape Cod.

197—The Hyannis Inn, Hyannis, Cape Cod, Mass.

5A-H1960

The Hyannis Inn protected
its guests from the summer
sun with colorful awnings.
[Postcard valued at $5-7]

Cape Codder Hotel, Falmouth, Cape Cod, Mass.

A veranda running along the entire front
façade of the Cape Codder allowed its
guests an excellent vantage point from
which to view the water below. [Postcard
valued at $4-6]

WYCHMERE HARBOR AND SNOW INN, HARWICHPORT, CAPE COD, MASS.

The Snow Inn placed its guests practically in the heart of harbor life in Harwichport. Today the building houses luxury condos. [Postcard valued at $3-5]

Despite the grandeur of resorts, there is something relaxing about a small cottage to oneself like these along Old Wharf Road in Dennisport. [Postcard valued at $3-5]

318—Cottages and Beach Along Old Wharf Road, Dennisport, Cape Cod, Mass.

2C-H1214

A SUMMER HOME ON THE CAPE, MASS.

Beautiful memories as well as flowers can blossom at a summer home on the Cape. The writer of this postcard sent it from "No. Eastham" in 1947. [Postcard valued at $4-6]

42105

225—Cottages at Swifts Beach, Cape Cod, Mass.

A more recent card postmarked 1960 shows visitors coming and going to the beach from their summer cottages at Swifts Beach. The card is postmarked 1960. [Postcard valued at $5-7]

6B-H1378

108018-N

For the budget-conscious, there are rooms to rent that place the visitor in the heart of Cape Cod neighborhoods as in this scene of picturesque Provincetown. [Postcard valued at $4-6]

The Year-Rounders

"Old Dan'l Hanks he says his town
Is jest the best on earth;
He says there ain't one, up nor down,
That's got one half her worth;
He says there ain't no other state
That's good as ourn, nor near;
And all the folks that's good and great
Is settled right 'round here."

– From "The Village Oracle"

Cape Codders have the luxury of enjoying the Cape year-round, or so it would seem to visitors who leave the place only begrudgingly to go home to their regular routines once again. But those who live on the Cape also lead lives that are routine to them, if not made more pleasurable by the beauty of their surroundings.

Many live in a style of house named for their "homeland." They go to work, school, and church to the tidal rhythm of the seas. In their varied occupations, they serve not only their neighbors, but also the burgeoning influx of tourists with a welcome as warm as the sun on a summer beach.

Some characteristics of a Cape Cod style home are the pitched roof to allow snow to slide off and the central chimney to radiate heat to all the rooms. Card is postmarked 1937. [Postcard valued at $3-5]

Current Cape Cod house plans are based on a revival of American Colonial design and are New England's biggest contribution to American architecture. This charming card is postmarked 1915. [Postcard valued at $3-5]

126   Homes By the Sea, Cape Cod, Mass.

4A-H2039

The home's low profile helped protect it from the winds and rains along the Cape. This scene of a home by the sea is postmarked 1958. [Postcard valued at $3-5]

Originally these homes were built in protected spots, usually facing South to get the full benefit of the sun. The scene in this card, postmarked 1928, was taken on the road from Falmouth to Sandwich. [Postcard valued at $2-4]

124.   AN OLD CAPE COD HOUSE, CAPE COD, MASS.   86474

A Quaint Old Home on Cape Cod, Mass.

31

103—An Old House (Built in 1752), Cape Cod, Mass.

4B-H955

Another advantage to this style home was that it could grow with the family. Often a small "half house" was built first. The half Cape is characterized today as a section of house front that has a door with two windows on one side. When more room was needed, the house could be enlarged to a "three-quarter Cape" or a "house-and-a-half," with two windows on one side of the door and one on the other, or a full Cape with two windows on each side of the door. The larger home shown here is the old Atwood House in Chatham that was built in 1752.
[Postcards valued at $3-5 each]

A different roof style, such as a rare bow or gambrel roof, could indicate that the home was originally built by a ship builder. [Postcard valued at $4-6]

AN OLD CAPE COD HOUSE, BUILT 1750.

207 AN OLD HOUSE (BUILT 1792), CAPE COD. MASS.

9-2123

The Cape Cod house also allowed for expansion upward, so that a storage attic could be turned into extra sleeping quarters. This card features a home built in 1792 and is postmarked 1939. [Postcard valued at $4-6]

Joshua Crosby's House, Tonset, Cape Cod, Mass.

LC4

(Photo by Hicks)

76204

Being a frame structure, the traditional Cape Cod house has siding left to weather gracefully as on the Tonset, Cape Cod, house of Joshua Crosby who was once the keeper of the Nauset Light. [Postcard valued at $3-5]

Sometimes glass transoms and dormers help to light the interiors of Cape Cod houses. Card is postmarked 1943. [Postcard valued at $3-5]

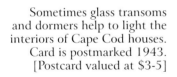

An Old House on Cape Cod, Mass.

35

AN OLD CAPE COD HOUSE. BUILT 1713. CAPE COD. MASS.   16

The Howes House in Dennis was built in 1713. Many tiny panes of glass in the windows reflect the Cape sunshine. This card is postmarked 1941. [Postcard valued at $3-5]

127   AN EARLY CAPE COD HOUSE   72749

In a card postmarked 1940, a Cape Cod house by the sea is colored like the sky and water surrounding it. *"It stands at the bend where the road has its end, / And the blackberries nod on the vine; / And the sun flickers down to its gables of brown, / Through the sweet-scented boughs of the pine."* From "The Little Old House by the Sea." [Postcard valued at $3-5]

Labeled simply as "Aunt Hannah's," this Cape Cod on the King's Highway "grew" front-to-back rather than side-to-side. The card is postmarked 1921. [Postcard valued at $3-5]

126.   A TYPICAL CAPE COD HOUSE.   96789

WINDY WILLOWS, CAPE COD, MASS.

42732

This Cape Cod is situated on Corn Hill. Here, with their ship anchored in what is now Provincetown Harbor, an exploratory party of Pilgrims discovered the store of corn natives had put away for the winter. The pilgrim's decided it was Divine Providence that led them to the corn and prevented their starvation. Card is postmarked 1941. [Postcard valued at $3-5]

168   *An Old Cape Cod Home, Cape Cod, Mass.*

5B-H853

Merchants and sea captains began to build more elaborate homes with a full second story as they acquired wealth. The image for this postcard was taken on Route 6A at Yarmouthport. [Postcard valued at $4-6]

Old House with Famous "Widow's Walk," Cape Cod, Mass.   66

A home with a "widow's walk" dates from the old Cape Cod sailing vessel days and was undoubtedly the home of a seafaring man. From its height, the woman of the household could watch for the return of her husband's ship. Even if it was lost at sea, often she would continue to watch faithfully for the phantom ship that never came: *"Yet well he knows – where'er it be, / On low Cape Cod or bluff Cape Ann – / With straining eyes that search the sea, / A watching woman waits her man...."* From "The Cod-Fisher." [Postcard valued at $5-7]

(Photo by Hicks)   76269

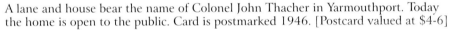

A lane and house bear the name of Colonel John Thacher in Yarmouthport. Today the home is open to the public. Card is postmarked 1946. [Postcard valued at $4-6]

The Dillingham House was built around 1659. Legend states that John Dillingham used bricks and other materials that had come from England as ballast on a ship. The rear of the home features the long, sweeping roofline of a saltbox style home. Card is postmarked 1935. [Postcard valued at $3-5]

As the postcard states, this charming Cape Cod home is "a cottage by the side of the road." Card is postmarked 1944. [Postcard valued at $3-5]

135　A TYPICAL CAPE COD HOME, CAPE COD, MASS.

129—An Old Cape Cod Home

Part of the charm of Cape Cod homes are the picket fences over which neighbors chat, flowers trail, and guests pass through. These cards' images were taken in Centerville and Harwichport respectively. [Postcard values: top $4-6; bottom $3-5]

A DOORWAY OF AN OLD CAPE COD HOUSE, MASS.

A CAPE COD FIREPLACE.

With a long history of Americana tradition, many Cape Cod homes are filled with antiques. This postcard features a Cape Cod fireplace. [Postcard valued at $4-6]

Enter into a Cape Cod home and the charm continues. There are treasures to discover: a display of Sandwich glass in a sunny window, scrimshaw work set atop the mantle, and Grandmother's braided rug in front of the hearth. This postcard features the door of the old Dillingham House in Brewster. [Postcard valued at $5-7]

The hearth truly is the heart of a Cape Cod home. Some brick fireplaces also had ovens so that the hearth became a place to heat, illuminate, and feed the family. Card is postmarked 1943. [Postcard valued at $4-6]

64:- AN EARLY FIREPLACE, CAPE COD, MASS.

"I like it best inside, with the fire a-gleamin', / And myself, with chores all done, settin' round and dreamin', / With the kitten on my knee, and the kettle hummin', / And the rain-drops on the roof, / 'Home, Sweet Home' a-drummin'." From "A Rainy Day." Card is postmarked 1950. [Postcard valued at $4-6]

204—Main Street, Falmouth, Cape Cod, Mass.

Main Street Looking East, Hyannis, Mass.   H21

Cape Codders work and play in the many villages that comprise the towns. Main streets are lined with shops, banks, offices, and government buildings. Here are the main streets of Hyannis and Falmouth respectively as they appeared decades ago. [Postcard values: left $9-11; right $10-12]

1117—Cape Cod Hospital, Cape Cod, Mass.

OC-H1531

Hospitals care for both those who live on Cape Cod and those unfortunate enough to take ill on vacation. The hospital in Hyannis was rebuilt in 1950 with funds raised by popular subscription. Card is postmarked 1958. [Postcard valued at $7-9]

Communities revolve around their public buildings, such as post offices. Here is the post office at Hyannis. Card is postmarked 1949. [Postcard valued at $5-7]

H14   Post Office and Town Hall, Hyannis, Cape Cod, Mass.

The Hyannis Public Library is near the post office at 401 Main Street. [Postcard valued at $4-6]

PHOTOGRAPH BY HARRISON FISK

OB-H1870

TOWN HALL AND SOLDIERS' MONUMENT, BOURNE.

Courthouses and Town Halls throughout Cape Cod are often crowned with steeples much like the area's churches. Here is an early view of the Town Hall in Bourne with the Soldiers' Monument standing proudly nearby. Card is postmarked 1929. [Postcard valued at $6-8]

1102—State Teachers' College, Hyannis, Cape Cod, Mass.

PHOTOGRAPH BY HARRISON FISK

OB-H1873

The State Teachers' College in Hyannis became the old Maritime Academy. *"...And so he dreamed, with a happy face, / Till the noontide recess came, / And when 't was over, ah, sad disgrace, / The teacher, seeing an empty place, / Marked 'truant' against his name; / While he, forgetful of book or rule, / Sought only a tree to climb: / For where is the boy who remembers school, / When the cowslip blows by the marshy pool, / And it's just birds'-nesting time?"* From "Birds'-Nesting Time." [Postcard valued at $4-6]

SEA PINES SCHOOL, EAST BREWSTER, CAPE COD, MASS.

This postcard shows the Sea Pines School, which was originally founded in 1907 as the Sea Pines School of Charm and Personality for Young Women, and now offers lodging to tourists as the Old Sea Pines Inn in Brewster. Card is postmarked 1932. [Postcard valued at $5-7]

Mac Arnold's Lobster Pound on the Canal, Bourne, Cape Cod, Mass.

126

77445

(Photo by Hicks)

THE LOBSTER POUND NEAR THE NEW BOURNE BRIDGE ON CAPE COD CANAL. MASS.

61420

Restaurants are favorite gathering places where natives and tourists alike come to enjoy Cape Cod's famous fresh seafood. Many sport sea-themed names like old MacArnold's Lobster Pound in Bourne along the Cape Cod Canal. The second view shows the Bourne Bridge in the background. [Postcards valued at $3-5 each]

Our house is on a hill in back of this bay, looking down on it.

A view of the Woods Hole waterfront shows the Oceanographic Institute, the Marine Biological Laboratory, and the U.S. Fisheries Building in the background. The Institute emphasizes exploration of the oceans' depths. Its belled cupola and brass weathervane have become landmarks. [Postcard valued at $3-5]

MARINE BIOLOGICAL LABORATORY BUILDING. WOODS HOLE, CAPE COD, MASS.

Many Cape Cod careers revolve around the seas. Nowhere is this more evident than in Woods Hole, where the Marine Biological Laboratory was established as early as 1888. Today, its presence encompasses most of the lower two-thirds of Water Street. [Postcard valued at $4-6]

178—Oldest Baptist Church on Cape Code, Mass.

The week closes with the Sabbath as locals flock to places of worship of all denominations. Here a Baptist church built in 1769 lifts its white spire to the heavens in the tradition of so many New England churches. [Postcard valued at $4-6]

A CROSSROAD, PROVINCETOWN, CAPE COD, MASS.

UNIVERSALIST CHURCH TOWER, DESIGNED BY CHRISTOPHER WREN.

Green and Congregational Church, Falmouth, Cape Cod, Mass.

A typical picturesque Cape Cod scene is the village green setting for a white-steepled church. This card featuring the Congregational Church in Falmouth is postmarked 1944. [Postcard valued at $4-6]

The Universalist Church tower designed by architect Christopher Wren stands sentinel in Provincetown. Card is postmarked 1948. [Postcard valued at $3-5]

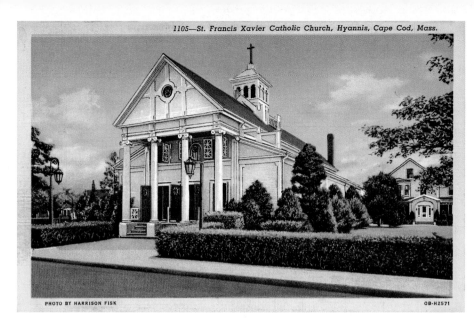

1105—St. Francis Xavier Catholic Church, Hyannis, Cape Cod, Mass.

PHOTO BY HARRISON FISK   0B-H2571

1105—St. Francis Xavier Catholic Church, Hyannis. Cape Cod, Mass.

6B-H1741

John F. Kennedy and his brothers were all altar boys at St. Francis Xavier Catholic Church in Hyannis. [Postcard values: top left $4-6; top right $3-5; bottom $4-6]

1123— Federated Church, Hyannis, Cape Cod, Mass.

4B-H1063

Another church from Hyannis is the Federated Church. [Postcard valued at $4-6]

135—Holy Trinity Catholic Church, Cape Cod, Mass.

4B-H952

There are some thirty denominations represented on Cape Cod. This card of Holy Trinity Catholic Church in West Harwich is postmarked 1960. [Postcard valued at $4-6]

The vine-covered façade and lush plantings around many Cape Cod churches allow them to nestle peacefully into residential areas. Here is a view of Our Lady of Lourdes Church in Wellfleet. [Postcard valued at $4-6]

Our Lady of Lourdes Church, Wellfleet, Cape Cod, Mass.   LC21

(Photo by Hicks)

76246

1109— St. Andrews-by-the-Sea, Hyannisport, Cape Cod, Mass.

PHOTO BY HARRISON FISK

8A-H2919

St. Andrews-by-the-Sea rests on Sunset Hill, one of the highest points on the Cape. Card is postmarked 1961. [Postcard valued at $3-5]

THE OLD INDIAN CHURCH, MASHPEE, CAPE COD, MASS.

44717

The oldest church building on Cape Cod is the Old Indian Meeting House at Mashpee. This little church was completely renovated in 1970. Its simplicity is comforting. [Postcard valued at $4-6]

"THE ANGELUS," WOODS HOLE, CAPE COD, MASS.

47825

"The Angelus" at Woods Hole inspired this postcard. *From the window of the chapel softly sounds an organ's note, / Through the wintry, Sabbath gloaming, drifting shreds of music float....* From "Sunday Afternoons." [Postcard valued at $3-5]

Cape Cod's Picture-Book Beauty

"Come in the glow of the olden days,
Come with a youthful face,
Come through the old familiar ways,
Up from the dear, old place.
Barefoot, trip through the meadow lane,
Laughing at bruise and scratch;
Come, with your hands all rich with stain
Fresh from the blackberry patch."

– From "Grandfather's "Summer Sweets"

Cape Cod's landscape is a combination of rugged rocky coastlines, windswept beaches, salty marshes, and flower-strewn fields. Traveling the Cape's highways and back roads provides a kaleidoscope of colors and forms. Each curve in the road seems to bring another "aah-inspiring" view.

One of the best souvenirs of visits to the Cape has been the simple postcard. It captures a thumbnail sketch of a time and place now once removed. On its reverse side, many a tourist has waxed poetic about places and people that the recipient read with longing and, perhaps, reminiscences of his own. Thank goodness for these "mailable master-pieces," and for those who have lovingly preserved them in family albums and scrapbooks throughout the years for future generations to enjoy!

1111—The Harbor, Hyannis, Cape Cod, Mass.

1B-H175Z

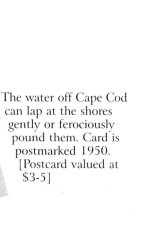

171—The Seashore on Cape Cod, Mass.

I Love To Walk By The Seashore

I love to walk by the seashore.
On the clean white sand so bare.
I love to walk by the rippling waves
For I find refuge there.

When a white fog's in the air;
When a pallid mist o'shadows
the beach
And no breeze is stirring there.

I love to walk by the seashore,
And watch the waves in motion,
I love the sea in all its moods
For God made the mighty ocean.

By THEODORE R. ROWLEY

5A-H2014

The water off Cape Cod can lap at the shores gently or ferociously pound them. Card is postmarked 1950. [Postcard valued at $3-5]

The sunlight is reflected in the waters of Hyannis harbor in this card postmarked 1960. *"Oh, the song of the Sea – / The wonderful song of the Sea! / Like the far-off hum of a throbbing drum, / It steals through the night to me: / And my fancy wanders free, / To a little seaport town, / And a spot I knew, where the roses grew, / By a cottage small and brown; / And a child strayed up and down, / O'er hillock and beach and lea, / And crept at dark to his bed, to hark, / To the wonderful song of the Sea."* From "The Song of the Sea." [Postcard valued at $4-6]

Shipwreck, Cape Cod, Mass.

Shell seekers may come upon the skeletal remains of
shipwrecks half buried in the sand. [Postcard valued at $3-5]

121—A Beautiful Harbor View on Cape Cod, Mass.

Harbor scenes are as varied as the towns that embrace them.
[Postcards valued at $4-6 each]

The inner harbor at Hyannis.

208 INNER HARBOR, HYANNIS, CAPE COD, MASS.

Pleasure boats in Falmouth Harbor.
[Postcard valued at $5-7]

Stage Harbor at Chatham.

Card postmarked 1940 shows the end of Grey Neck Road in Harwichport. *"When the tide goes out, how the foam flakes dance, / Through the wiry sedge-grass near the shore; / How the ripples spark in the sunbeam's glance, / As they madly tumble the pebbles o'er!"* From *"When the Tide Goes Out."* [Postcard valued at $3-5]

1114 —Excursion Boat in Hyannis Harbor, Cape Cod, Mass.

OC-H1530

Passengers on an excursion boat in Hyannis Harbor enjoying the scenery become part of the scenery themselves. [Postcard valued at $4-6]

Boaters and swimmers are not the only ones to enjoy the waters off Cape Cod. [Postcard valued at $2-4]

SEA GULLS ON THE BEACH, PROVINCETOWN, CAPE COD, MASS.

42103

BARGES ASHORE, PROVINCETOWN, CAPE COD, MASS.

Boats, once the backbone of the Cape's economy, can be found on land and sea – sailing, anchored, or dry-docked. Card is postmarked 1934. [Postcard valued at $3-5]

136—An Old Homestead, Cape Cod, Mass.

"The pine-clad hill has a crimson crown of glittering sunset glows; / The roofs of brown in the distant town are bathed in a blush of rose...." From "At Eventide." Card is postmarked 1950. [Postcard valued at $4-6]

4A-H711

105

56:—WAGON WHEELS ON CAPE COD DUNES, CAPE COD, MASS.

45309

Nothing adds to the beauty of a scene quite like a radiant sunset. Here it tinges the skies above Cape Cod dunes. [Postcard valued at $2-4]

Twilight descends upon Little Harbor in Woods Hole. [Postcard valued at $3-5]

LITTLE HARBOR. WOODS HOLE. CAPE COD, MASS.

39955

OSTERVILLE HARBOR. CAPE COD. MASS.

42048

The setting sun crowns the treetops around Osterville Harbor. [Postcard valued at $4-6]

Evening Salute at Camp Edwards, Mass., on Cape Cod

E8

The canons fire during evening salute at Camp Edwards on Cape Cod. [Postcard valued at $4-6]

70471

1112—Lewis Bay and Englewood Beach, Cape Cod, Mass.

6A-H2739

1101—View of Lewis Bay, Hyannis, Cape Cod, Mass.

OB-H1875

PHOTOGRAPH BY HARRISON FISK

Boats make for shore at the close of day along Englewood Beach in Lewis Bay. [Postcard valued at $3-5]

Another view of Lewis Bay at Hyannis is post-marked 1940. *"My dream-ship's decks are of beaten gold, / And her fluttering banners are brave of hue, / And her shining sails are of satin fold, / And her tall sides gleam where the warm waves woo: / While the flung spray leaps in a diamond dew, / From her bright bow, dipping its dance of glee; / For the skies are fair and the soft winds coo, / Where my dream-ship sails o'er the silver sea."* From "The Ballad of the Dream-Ship." [Postcard valued at $3-5]

General View of Mill Pond, Chatham, Cape Cod, Mass.

Besides the coastal waters, there are over 250 natural lakes and ponds throughout Cape Cod. Here is Mill Pond at Chatham. [Postcard valued at $4-6]

194—A Village Scene, Cape Cod, Mass.

4B-H947

154—Bass River Bridge, Cape Cod, Mass.

4B-H1070

The linen-white of sails and bridge stunningly contrast against the blues and greens of water, sky, and plants in this view of the Bass River Bridge on Route 28 that connects South Yarmouth with West Dennis. [Postcard valued at $3-5]

Entrance to Wellfleet Cape Cod, Mass.

Uncle Tim's Bridge provides a pedestrian path across Duck Creek and into the charming village of Wellfleet with its equally charming entrance. [Postcard values: top $3-5; bottom $4-6]

Views taken from the air often give a
breathtaking view of the seas.

139—Aeroplane View of Harwich Port, Cape Cod, Mass.

OB-H2572

© E. D. WEST CO.

Aerial view of Harwich Port. [Postcard valued at $4-6]

1119—Air View of Lewis Bay, Hyannis, Cape Cod, Mass.

PHOTO BY KELSEY, CHATHAM, MASS.

7B-H1299

Aerial view of Lewis Bay, Hyannis. [Postcard valued at $4-6]

27

HOLLYHOCK LANE AT PROVINCETOWN ON HISTORIC CAPE COD

Flowers run riot over the Cape in the summer as in Hollyhock Lane in Provincetown. [Postcard valued at $4-6]

Ramblers of Chatham, Cape Cod, Mass.

One of the Many Rose Covered Cottages on Cape Cod, Mass.

79499

Climbers like morning glories, clematis, and roses provide a fragrant mantle over Cape Cod fences, arbors, and rooflines. [Postcard values: top $4-6; bottom $3-5]

140—An Old Cape Cod Lane

5A-H2013

This card postmarked 1944 shows a scene from the old King's Highway at Yarmouthport. *"Down the lane, behind the orchard, where the wild rose blushes sweet, / Through the pasture, past the spring behind the brook, / Where the clover blossoms press their dewy kisses on my feet, / And the honeysuckle scents each shady nook; / By the meadow and the bushes, where the blackbirds build their nests, / Up the hill, beneath the shadow of the pine, / Till the breath of Ocean meets us, dancing o'er his sparkling crests, / And our faces feel the tingling of the brine."* From "The Meadow Road." [Postcard valued at $3-5]

Studio Gardens, Provincetown, Cape Cod, Mass.

Also abloom are the Studio Gardens of Provincetown. [Postcard valued at $4-6]

STONE ALLEY, CAPE COD, MASS.

The caption on this card is simply "Stone Alley, Cape Cod, Mass." *"How the mignonette's sweet blooming was perfuming all the walks, / Where the hollyhocks stood proudly with their blossom-dotted stalks; / While the old-maids' pinks were nodding groups of gossips, here and there, / And the bluebells swung so lightly in the lazy, hazy air!"* From "The Old-Fashioned Garden." [Postcard valued at $3-5]

117

CAPE COD, MASS.

I'm going back to the Cape;
Where salt waves greet the pine,
And battered sea hulks drape
Their arms in the ocean's brine.

Where glint of silver sail
Against a turquoise sea,
Or droning bell-buoy's wail
Hold a breath of ecstasy.

I'm going back again
Where tangy breezes blow,
And hark to fishermen
Tell tales of long ago.

Beside a weathered shack,
As waves salute the shore,
And gaunt trees stand forth black,
Cape Cod calls me once more.

Marjorie Bassett

7A-H2518

Flowers' fragrances mingle with the salty breezes off the Cape Cod coast to perfume the summer air.
[Postcard valued at $3-5]

946 Up-Along West End, Provincetown, Mass.

Cape Cod roads ramble up and down, or in the case of these sections of Provincetown, they ramble "Up-*Along*." [Postcard values: top $5-7; bottom $4-6]

STREET SCENE. "WAY UP ALONG." PROVINCETOWN. CAPE COD. MASS.

Sand and Pines, Cape Cod Mass.

113

(Photo by Hicks)

76261

Not all roads lead through civilization. Others reveal stretches of sand, beach grass, and pines. [Postcard valued at $2-4]

149—State Road across the Sand Dunes, Cape Cod, Mass.

1A40-N

Here the State Road runs through the uninhabited sand dunes. [Postcard valued at $2-4]

143—Sand Dunes, Cape Cod, Mass.

Winds have shaped much of Cape Cod's landscape and even the vegetation as a lone, bent tree crops up among the dunes now and then like a giant's bonsai. [Postcard valued at $2-4]

95659-N

141—Cape Cod Sand Dunes

A visitor's tracks and footprints have a short life-span on the shifting sands of Cape Cod. [Postcard valued at $2-4]

61144-N

142. Cape Cod Sand Dunes

5B-H856

Fierce gale winds can swirl the Cape's sand dunes into rippled pinnacles or polish them
into smooth, shiny mounds. Card is postmarked 1947. [Postcard valued at $2-4]

Cape Cod Landscape

(Photo by Hicks)

76254

A Cape Cod village can often be found nestled among the fields and woodlands from the vantage point of an elevated road. Card is postmarked 1949. [Postcard valued at $3-5]

LEWIS BAY, HYANNIS, CAPE COD, MASS.

39939

© HOWARD

Here is a colorful scenes from Lewis Bay. *"See the shadow and the shine, / Where the glossy branches twine, / And the ocean's sleepy tuning mocks the crooning in the pine; / Hear the catbird whistle shrill, / In the bushes by the rill, / Where the violets toss and twinkle as they sprinkle vale and hill...."* From "May Memories." [Postcard valued at $3-5]

MARSH SCENE, CAPE COD, MASS.

39911

As seen in this card postmarked 1940, travels along Cape Cod can reveal a lone gem of a cottage...

...or a necklace of cozy dwellings strung along sandy lanes as at Mill Point. [Postcard values: top $3-5; bottom $4-6]

Wind Mill at old Mill Point, Cape Cod, Mass.

Cape Cod gave its name to a style of home that is simple yet cozy. Cape Cod style homes can be found along the shore or inland on country roads where moist, salt-laden winds help hasten their facades to a weathered patina. [Postcard valued at $4-6]

An old mill in Sandwich is reflected in water as clear as the glass pressed into patterns of cup plates that have become the town's signature. Card is postmarked 1937. [Postcard valued at $3-5]

"Feel the tangled meadow-grass, / On my bare feet as I pass; / See the clover bending over, / In a dew-bespangled mass; / See the cottage by the shore, / With the pansy beds before, / And the old familiar places and the faces at the door." From "May Memories." [Postcard valued at $3-5]

Quaint Cape Cod Scene. Cape Cod, Mass.

19

61295

69:–AN OLD CAPE COD GRIST MILL. CAPE COD, MASS.

42104

An arbor gracefully frames an old Cape Cod gristmill. [Postcard valued at $4-6]

PICTURESQUE CAPE COD, MASS.

Windmills along the marshes were used to pump up seawater to be dried in large
wooden vats for making salt. Card is postmarked 1937. [Postcard valued at $3-5]

Old Windmill, Cape Cod, Mass.

109—Oldest Wind Mill on Cape Cod, Mass.

Their original use long since abandoned, windmills now model for photographers and painters from shoreline to meadows. [Postcards valued at $3-5 each]

CAPE COD SCENE NEAR HYANNIS, CAPE COD, MASS.

111721

Anyone who has ever seen Cape Cod will long remember it for its wealth of colors and textures, of sights, aromas, and sounds. There is something there to please everyone and every sense. Each comes away with his or her favorite scenes. This picturesque scene is near Hyannis. [Postcard valued at $3-5]